Prototyping

CHERRY LAKE PUBLISHING • ANN ARBOR, MICHIGAN

by Eric Cook

308.04 1506

R

A Note to Adults: Please review the instructions for the activities in this book before allowing children to do them. Be sure to help them with any activities you do not think they can safely complete on their own.

CHERRY LAKE
Publishing

A Note to Kids: Be sure to ask an adult for help with these activities when you need it. Always put your safety first!

Published in the United States of America by Cherry Lake Publishing
Ann Arbor, Michigan
www.cherrylakepublishing.com

Series editor: Kristin Fontichiaro

Photo Credits: Cover and page 1, Waag Society / tinyurl.com/le36b8r / CC-BY-2.0; page 5, sandy Poore / tinyurl.com/le36b8r / CC-BY-SA 2.0; page 7, russellstreet / tinyurl.com/no9jpe8 / CC-BY-SA-2.0; page 9, Mvuijlst / tinyurl.com/puz89ww / Public Domain; page 11, Windgeist / tinyurl.com/l6tznbe / CC-BY-SA-2.0; page 15, breki74 / tinyurl.com/mzzd2f2 / CC-BY-SA-2.0; page 16, Steve Jurvetson / tinyurl.com/k357pux / CC-BY-2.0; page 21, Peter Merholz / tinyurl.com/lnq56bu / CC-BY-SA-2.0; page 22, NASA Goddard Space Flight Center / tinyurl.com/omftqpd / CC-BY-2.0; page 24, Samuel Mann / tinyurl.com/muhddvs / CC-BY-2.0; page 27, Creative Tools / tinyurl.com/mgabd99 / CC-BY-2.0; page 29, Jeffrey Putney / tinyurl.com/kdxrlbu / CC-BY-2.0.

Library of Congress Cataloging-in-Publication Data
Cook, Eric,
 1971– Prototyping / by Eric Cook.
   pages cm. — [21st century skills innovation library] [Makers as innovators]
 Audience: Grades 4 to 6.
 Includes bibliographical references and index.
 ISBN 978-1-63188-869-4 [lib. bdg.] — ISBN 978-1-63188-893-9 (pdf) — ISBN 978-1-63188-881-6 (pbk.) —ISBN 978-1-63188-905-9 (e-book)
 1. Prototypes, Engineering—Juvenile literature. I. Title.
 TS171.8.C66 2015
 620'.0042—dc23   2014029096

Cherry Lake Publishing would like to acknowledge the work of The Partnership for 21st Century Skills. Please visit www.p21.org for more information.

Printed in the United States of America
Corporate Graphics Inc.
January 2015

Contents

Chapter 1   **What Is Prototyping?**   4

Chapter 2   **Why Prototype?**   9

Chapter 3   **The Process of Prototyping**   15

Chapter 4   **Evaluating and Revising**   22

Glossary   30

Find Out More   31

Index   32

About the Author   32

Chapter 1

What Is Prototyping?

What if your parents said, "Do your homework, but make sure you don't finish it!" Imagine if your teacher told you, "Don't spend too much time on your assignment, because you'll just wind up changing it later." These might seem like crazy things to say. However, there are times when they are exactly what you should do! Learning to build quick, unfinished drafts of your ideas is an important part of becoming a more effective **maker**. We even give this process a special name—**prototyping**.

Prototyping means making a rough draft of an idea so you can test it out. An artist might draw sketches in pencil before taking the time to make a big painting. Similarly, makers create prototypes to evaluate their designs, show ideas to other people, and think through problems before it is too late to make changes. Like an artist's sketches, prototypes are quick, sloppy, and easy to throw away if they don't turn out right.

Even simple materials such as colored paper and sticky notes can be used to create useful prototypes.

Prototypes can be created with any kind of tools and materials you have at hand, from simple paper or sticky notes to specialized computer software. In this book, you'll learn about some common techniques for prototyping. You'll also find out what makes these methods useful. With these tools in your kit, you'll be a more effective designer and maker—whether you're trying to create a Web site, a 3D model, a robot butler, or anything else.

Let's get started by meeting two makers, named Shona and Leo. They will each be working on their own projects. They'll provide examples of the value of prototyping. They will also show different parts of the prototyping process.

Shona's Big Idea

After watching a demo of a 3D printer at her local **makerspace**, Shona started thinking about how neat it would be to make custom jewelry for the kids in her school. She remembered that two of her classmates, Susan and Miles, had bought necklaces with each other's names on them to show their friendship. But Shona thought the necklaces would be even better if each one had *both* friends' names on it.

This idea of friendship necklaces was exciting to Shona. With a plan in mind, she started drawing sketches to show what the necklaces might look like. She hoped to show the sketches to the other kids in her class and see what they thought about her idea.

Leo's Big Idea

Leo loved pizza. He ordered online from his local favorite, Perry's Pizza Palace, as often as he could. But while Perry's made delicious pizza, there was one thing Leo didn't like about ordering—Perry's old, clunky Web site. One day, Leo complained about the site to his older sister Sylvie. "It's hard to see which toppings you've picked," he said. "I can never get more than three toppings at a time, and the whole site looks like it was made before I was born."

Sylvie rolled her eyes. "If it bugs you so much, why don't you design something better?" she asked.

"Maybe I will," Leo replied. Soon, visions of pepperoni began to fill his head . . .

Leo's difficulties ordering pizza are inspiring him to make something new.

What Prototypes Are and Aren't

Prototypes are:

- Cheap
- Disposable
- A step in a larger process of making

This means prototypes are created quickly and thrown away—on purpose!—as part of generating and testing your ideas.

Prototypes aren't:

- Finished projects
- Something that has to be done on a computer
- Only used to design one kind of thing. Designers use prototypes to build computer programs, Web sites, and games. They are also used to make things like furniture, electronics, toys, and much more.

Chapter 2

Why Prototype?

One of the first questions you might have is, why
bother? That is, why take the time to make a
prototype (let alone several of them) when you
could jump right into making the real thing? Good
question! There are two big reasons why prototyping
works better than treating your first design as your
final design.

The first reason
is that prototyp-
ing allows you to
improve your ideas.
As you work on a
prototype, you will
repeat the design
process several
times. Each time,
you will come up
with more ideas to
improve your proj-
ect. In professional

Prototyping has helped inventors such as
Thomas Edison to create some of history's
most important devices, such as the light bulb.

9

terms, this is called **iterative design**. Nobody gets a project right on the first try. Trying something over and over is a key part of generating great results. When he was creating the electric lightbulb, inventor Thomas Edison tested out more than 1,600 different filaments (the part of the bulb that lights up) before settling on the right one! You don't need to come up with that many versions of your design, but you'll learn surprising things when you avoid settling on your first idea.

If you're coming up with a lot of ideas, you shouldn't get too attached to any of them right off the bat. You also shouldn't invest too much time in any single one of them at first. This is why prototypes should be cheap and disposable. You shouldn't be afraid to throw a design away if it isn't doing the job. This just means you can move on to different ideas while there is still time to change them.

The second big reason prototyping is a good idea is because it allows you to communicate your ideas to other people. The idea in your head may make sense to you, but it is just imaginary until you build a prototype. Despite the image of the inventor alone in his lab often seen in movies, real making is done with and for

Makerspaces are filled with supplies and tools that can help you with your projects.

others. You may have collaborators, such as an artist friend who works on the graphics and images for your project. You may be building your invention at a makerspace, where you can get help with special tools like a 3D printer or a laser cutter. By showing your collaborator a specific prototype, rather than describing a general concept, you're making sure that you are both viewing the problem in the same way. That way, the two of you won't try to accomplish different things at the same time.

In a way, prototypes also help you communicate with yourself. By making your ideas concrete, you

Design Thinking

Iterative prototyping is often used as part of user-centered design, also called design thinking. This approach to design encourages makers to think about who will use the things they are making, what they are trying to accomplish, and where their inventions will be used. This might seems like common sense. For a long time, however, designers usually assumed either that they knew exactly what people needed or that the users of their designs needed and wanted the same things the inventors did. As it turns out, this is often not the case!

Iterative prototyping helps you test with real users to make sure that what you're building actually suits their needs. User-centered design also encourages makers to create personas (imaginary people), scenarios (imaginary settings), and storyboards (drawings showing how a product will be used) to help them focus on users.

can remember details, keep better track of different options for your design, and do more effective comparisons between different ideas. Makers often use notebooks, sketch pads, and idea journals. These are other ways of capturing your prototypes so you can look back at them later!

Shona's Project

Shona showed her sketches of customized friendship necklaces to the kids at her lunch table. They really liked the idea. Their comments about the project gave Shona some new ideas that she hadn't originally considered. The idea she liked best was to have each half of the friendship necklace be a separate piece. That way, kids could easily snap together different necklaces with several different friends.

Before using time and materials to start making necklaces on a 3D printer, Shona decided to prototype her idea using string, LEGO pieces, and name stickers. That way, the kids at lunch could actually try snapping the pieces together and trading necklace halves.

Leo's Project

Leo decided to prototype his new pizza ordering system on paper. He learned a little about making Web sites at the computer camp he attended the previous summer, but drawing his ideas on paper was quicker than actually building a site. It also let him try out ideas that were beyond his level of Web design knowledge. Fortunately, Sylvie had learned about more advanced Web design in her computer classes at school. She agreed to help make Leo's final design actually work!

Leo's idea for a new ordering system would allow users to drag pictures of the toppings they wanted onto an image of a pizza. Leo was excited about how fun and quick this would be. The system could show different pizza sizes, amounts of toppings, and more. To prototype this idea, Leo drew a sketch of what the Web site might look like. He also made pictures of toppings using sticky notes so they could easily be moved around. When he tested the idea on his friends, he planned to have them talk out loud about what they are doing with the system. By telling him what they were thinking—and what was frustrating and con-fusing along the way—these testers would help him improve his design.

Chapter 3

The Process of Prototyping

By now you should understand the reasons why prototyping is so helpful. So how do you get started? How does prototyping actually work?

At first look, the process of prototyping seems straightforward. You start by creating simplified versions of your design. Then you use those creations to test and think about your design decisions. Don't try to do everything at once in an early prototype. Instead, think about

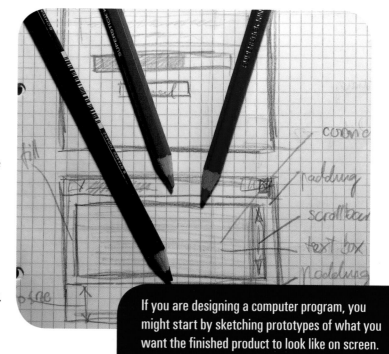

If you are designing a computer program, you might start by sketching prototypes of what you want the finished product to look like on screen.

which aspect of your invention you want to evaluate first. Focus your attention there for the moment.

Regardless of what they are trying to make, many designers rely on paper prototyping to develop their ideas before they start doing anything on the computer. In fact, a recent **survey** of professional

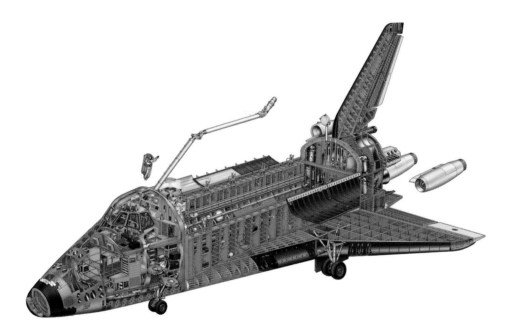

Once you've sketched out a paper prototype, a 3D computer model might be the next step. Even complex designs such as space shuttles are modeled in 3D before they are built.

Levels of Prototypes

Not all prototyping is done at the same level of detail. Here are some common levels of complexity you might hear designers talk about when they are discussing prototypes:

- Sketches:

    These are very rough drawings that are used to generate new ideas or explore a new approach.

- Low-fidelity:

    This is a stage of detail above initial sketching but still not concerned with specific visual details such as colors or **fonts**. Lo-fi prototypes are particularly useful for testing because they keep people focused on the big picture of your design instead of the little details.

- Wireframes:

    This is a medium level of complexity. It shows the spacing and location of different elements in the design.

- High-fidelity:

    This is the last stage of prototyping, when you're trying to make your design look realistic. It is useful for getting feedback on the little details that were avoided in the earlier stages.

The lines between these levels are fuzzy. One maker's low-fi prototype may be another maker's wireframe. The important thing to understand is that you'll make more versions at the early levels, where there is less detail. Less detail means less time and less commitment. These early stages should be the ones that are the cheapest and most disposable.

designers found that paper was their number one tool for prototyping. Paper is easy to find and simple to use. It is also a surprisingly flexible prototyping tool. You can draw, tape, overlap, and stick different pieces together to mock up most aspects of Web sites, mobile apps, and more. Try looking up "paper prototyping" on YouTube. You may be surprised by the number of clever uses that people have come up with for a simple piece of paper.

As useful as paper prototyping is, you will probably need to create your wireframes and high-fidelity prototypes on a computer. There are many programs and tools that can help you prototype different aspects of your idea, from the way it looks to the way people will use it. Some of these programs might already be on your computer. For example, you might have Microsoft Word and Microsoft PowerPoint, which can be used to create simple Web page prototypes. Other programs specially designed for prototyping (such as Axure) are less likely to be on your computer already. However, most software companies often provide less expensive or even free versions of their programs for students. See page 31

in this book for links to information about these programs and more.

Don't get bogged down worrying about whether
you're using the absolute "best" tool. There is no single right answer. The process of prototyping is very
flexible depending on your skills and the resources
available to you. What matters most is that you pick a
program that will do the things you want it to do.

Shona's Project

Shona's tests with her low-fidelity string-and-LEGO
necklaces were useful. She found out that people
thought they were either too small or too clunky. This
was discouraging at first, but it led Shona to think
about a different approach for her next round of
prototyping: Instead of necklaces, what about some
other kind of jewelry?

She hit on the idea of friendship bracelets, which
solved several issues. First, it seemed like clunky
shapes might be less of a concern with a bracelet.
Second, her test users in the lunchroom liked the idea
of being able to trade and collect pieces with more
than just one person at a time. Shona realized that a

large number of pieces would work better on a brace-let than a necklace.

Shona's shift in focus brought up some new questions, though. For instance, should the name pieces be charms that hang off the bracelet? Or should the names be printed on part of the bracelet itself? Shona started making another set of prototypes to try out these different options.

Leo's Project

When Leo first showed his sister Sylvie his sketches and drawings, he was a little surprised by the feedback she gave him. "These pepperoni look kind of weird," she said. "Maybe you should make them a different color of red than the tomato slices."

At first, Leo wondered why Sylvie was worried about something as simple as the color of pepperoni right now. Then he realized that he probably had put too much detail into the prototype he was showing her, at least for this stage of the process. He had been excited about the idea, so it had been fun to spend a lot of time drawing all the ingredients. But it also meant that Sylvie was paying more attention to his drawings than to the overall ideas about how the ordering system would work. With that in mind, Leo went back and drew a more simple set of black-and-white sketches for his design. They weren't as pretty, but he suspected they would help get the feedback he wanted right now.

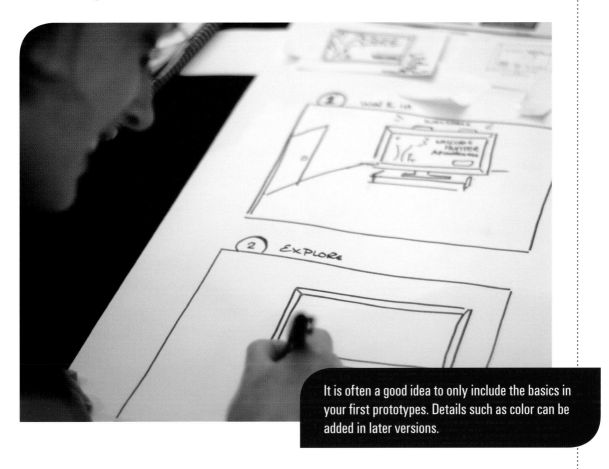

It is often a good idea to only include the basics in your first prototypes. Details such as color can be added in later versions.

Chapter 4

Evaluating and Revising

So you've made some prototypes for your design. But what do you do with them? As we've seen from Shona and Leo, you can use the prototypes to test your ideas and make changes. As mentioned earlier, prototyping is part of a larger process of design. This part of the process often goes something like this: prototype, evaluate, revise, evaluate, revise, evaluate, revise.

Even professional designers, like NASA scientists and engineers, must perform careful tests on their prototypes to make sure they will work properly in space. Here, they test a reflective material that protects spacecraft from the heat of the sun.

You can test many different things with your prototypes. So you should make sure that you know what you're trying to find out before you get started. Otherwise, the information you get from tests might not address your questions. Three main areas that you may want to evaluate with your prototypes are **functionality**, appeal, and appropriateness. Let's talk about each of these areas.

Evaluating functionality means asking, "How well does this design solve the problem?" and "How effective is it?" While this seems straightforward, there are different ways that design changes can be effective. For instance, did your improvements make the product faster than before? Is it less likely to cause mistakes? Is it less confusing?

While these questions are related, they aren't the same. Sometimes, improving one aspect of an invention actually makes another aspect worse! For example, there is often a trade-off to be made between speed and accuracy. When you do something very quickly, it is harder to do it correctly. Balancing the improvements in different kinds of functionality is a key job for a designer. When evaluating functionality, you need to decide what is most important and what kind of trade-offs you are willing to make.

A good way to evaluate different aspects of functionality is to set up a series of realistic tasks for your prototype. Then ask test users to work through those tasks. As they work, you might want to take measurements and record information about the prototype's functionality. For example, you might use a stopwatch to record how long it is taking testers to complete a task. You might also ask the testers to talk about

Talking to testers as they work with your prototype can help you see flaws you didn't notice at first.

what they are doing and thinking while they use the prototype. This will help you see your design from a different point of view.

The appeal of your prototype can be just as important as the effectiveness. Regardless of how well a device functions, people won't use it if they don't like it. The challenge here is that people can't always tell you what they do or don't like about a design. It may feel good to hear someone say, "I like it. It is nice!" However, this feedback does not help you figure out what to keep or change in the next revised prototype.

To gather information about which parts of a prototype people do or do not like, designers sometimes use survey questions. These questions allow designers to be very specific about what they want to know. Asking testers to talk out loud while they are testing a prototype and making note of when they are happy or upset can also be very informative.

Finally, a design needs to be appropriate. That means it needs to fit the people who are likely to use it as well as the times and places when it will be used. A phone application that reads texts from your friends in a loud, silly voice may be both functional and appealing, but if the intended setting for use is during class, it is not a very appropriate design solution!

Regardless of what you are evaluating, don't be afraid to ask what's wrong with your design. This is not a test that you are being graded on. In fact, finding out what isn't working right with your design and what people don't like about it are some of the most useful pieces of information you can get!

Shona's Project

After getting some more opinions, Shona decided that the bracelet should be made out of name pieces, rather than using charms. Her next design challenge was figuring out how to make this work. For the following round of prototyping, Shona began working with different kinds of latching connectors.

Eventually, she came up with something that seemed good-looking and easy to use. "Am I done?" she wondered. "I should probably do a round of hi-fi prototyping to make sure, before I start putting up posters all over the school advertising the bracelets."

Using a 3D printer, she made a sample bracelet and wore it for a few days. This turned out to be a

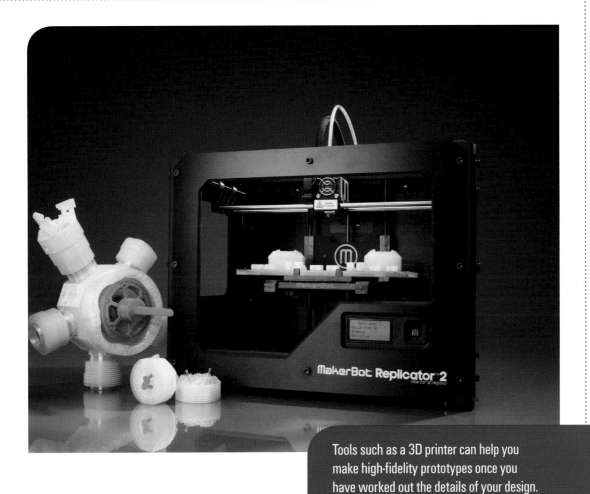

Tools such as a 3D printer can help you make high-fidelity prototypes once you have worked out the details of your design.

good idea. The bracelet was comfortable, and Shona got a lot of positive comments and questions when she wore it at school. But the hi-fi physical prototype also showed that the latches were not strong enough when made out of the 3D printer's plastic. They kept breaking off. This important detail needed to be fixed before Shona could call the project done.

Leo's Project

Once Leo revised his paper Web site prototype, he began to test it on more of his friends. These tests were very helpful for Leo. They emphasized the potential appeal of his design. As his friends moved different combinations of ingredients onto and off of the paper prototype, they laughed, made jokes with each other, and said things like, "This is so much fun!"

At the same time, the tests also pointed out several areas of possible confusion. For instance, if someone put pepperoni on just half of the pizza, did that mean they only wanted it on half or that they were just being sloppy as they dragged the ingredients over? What was the best way to show double orders of ingredients? A single layer of mushrooms didn't really look that different from a double layer in the paper version. And if someone wanted to order a pizza with nine different toppings, how could the designer be sure that all of the toppings were still visible? By raising additional questions and problems to be solved, the tests helped Leo think about how he needed to improve the design in the next version.

Visiting a makerspace or meeting with fellow makers can help you think of new ideas for inventions.

Wrapping Up

As you follow the prototyping process with your own designs, you will find that you're able to make better, more effective, and more appealing creations. You'll improve your skills as a maker, an inventor, and a designer.

What will you make next? With the right ideas and careful use of prototypes, almost anything will be possible!

Glossary

fonts (FAHNTS) styles of type

functionality (fuhngk-shuh-NA-luh-tee) a measurement of how useful or practical something is

iterative design (IT-ur-uh-tiv di-ZINE) the process of creating several versions of a project and improving it each time

maker (MAY-kur) someone who uses his or her creativity to make something

makerspace (MAY-kur-spays) a place containing tools and other equipment where makers can share ideas and work on projects

prototyping (PROH-tuh-tipe-ing) creating the first version of an invention that tests an idea to see if it will work

survey (SUR-vay) a study of the opinions or experiences of a group of people, based on their responses to questions

Find Out More

BOOKS

Fontichiaro, Kristin. *Design Thinking.* Ann Arbor, Michigan: Cherry Lake Publishing, 2015.

O'Neill, Terence, and Josh Williams. *3D Printing.* Ann Arbor, Michigan: Cherry Lake Publishing, 2014.

WEB SITES

Smashing Magazine
www.smashingmagazine.com/2010/03/29/free-printable-sketching-wireframing-and-note-taking-pdf-templates/
Check out this collection of helpful resources for creating many different types of paper prototypes.

Proto.io
http://proto.io/
Try out a free version of this useful prototyping software.

Index

appeal, 25, 28
appropriateness, 25–26

collaborators, 11, 12
communication, 10–13
computer programs, 18–19

feedback, 17, 19, 20, 21, 25, 26, 28
functionality, 23–24, 25

high-fidelity prototypes, 17, 18,
   26–27

iterative design, 10, 12

low-fidelity prototypes, 13, 17, 19

materials, 5, 13

paper prototyping, 14, 16, 18, 28

sketches, 4, 6, 13, 14, 16, 17, 18,
   20–21
survey questions, 25

testing, 4, 8, 10, 12, 13, 14, 15, 17,
   19–20, 22, 23, 24–25, 28
3D printers, 12, 26–27

wireframes, 17, 18

About the Author

A native of Michigan, Eric Cook is an academic, teacher, technologist, and musician. After spending more than a decade as a touring rock drummer, electronic music producer, and audio engineer, Cook earned an MSI in Human-Computer Interaction and a PhD in Information from the University of Michigan. A former lecturer and director of Undergraduate Programmes at University College Dublin's School of Information and Library Studies, Cook now teaches about interaction design and information in social systems at the University of Michigan's School of Information.